Makeover

Creating a balanced and fruitful life

BY BIMBO FOLA-ALADE

Published by

VISION MEDIA COMMUNICATIONS

Life MakeOver

Published by
Vision Media Communications
info@developingleaders.net
Tel: 07903 822 987
www.developingleaders.net

ISBN 978-0-9564767-2-2
Printed in the United Kingdom.

CONTENTS

Dedications

This book is dedicated to the men in my life - my husband and 2 sons.
You make every day a joy.

I love you.

Foreword

If anyone is well qualified to write a book on how to balance ones roles as a woman, it is definitely my dear Wife Abimbola. Over the years, I have thought of her as something of a "Superwoman" and wondered if she had superhuman strength. I have often wondered how she has been able to balance her very demanding roles and responsibilities as a loving wife and caring mother, self-less minister, teacher, writer, editor, counselor and occasional property developer!

She combines all this with a walk with God and many times without consistent domestic support; and most of the time she manages to remain her calm and sweet self! My wife is truly an example of a 21st century Proverbs 31 Woman in that, "She also rises while it is yet night and provides food for her household". Verses 15, 16, 23, 27-30 in particular describe her. In this book she shares practical tips and wisdom to help women balance the competing demands on their time and to build a fruitful and God honoring lifestyle.

She has ample experience from which to share with women about how to make life work. She continues to teach, lead and encourage hundreds of women through seminars and retreats, small group meetings, counseling and mentoring. I believe that when you read this book and apply the principles there in you will become the woman God intends for you to be - a Spirit Empowered and Fulfilled Woman, Wife and Mother.

Enjoy the read.

Dr. Sola Fola-Alade

PART 1

Life in the Fast Lane!

Makeover

The way we live

The 21st century woman is overcommitted, stressed and often at her wits end. We were raised believing we could have it all – a career, a happy marriage and children; but few of us realised how much it would take to have it all. 40% of British women with dependant children work over 30 hours a week, and another 40% work between 16-30 hours a week.

> *The 21st century woman is overcommitted, stressed and often at her wits end.*

27 per cent of women whose youngest child was aged 0-4 year's work 36 or more hours per week. The average UK woman then spends another seventeen and half hours per week on housework[2]. As a result many of us are under constant pressure, living with an eye to the clock.

The Office of National Statistics Time Use Survey[3] looked specifically at working women in Britain and what they do during a typical 24-hour period to create a typical "Diary of a Working Mum".

- Working women sleep less and work more than any other "type" of woman - and still have to do about two-and-a-half hours "domestic work" every day.

- A typical working woman gets nearly 40 minutes less sleep every night than a full-time mother who gets more than nine hours sleep every night.

- She gets up earlier to travel into work every day, or spends time every night doing a long list of domestic chores before going to bed.

Our partners also work long hours. 35 per cent of men work 46 hours or more a week, 20 per cent work 41-45 hours and 32 per cent work 36-40 hours[4]. As a result, we can rarely count on them to do much around the house; and

the constant mental pressure of trying to remember too many things and multi tasking to save time means we are living like pressure cookers. An architect friend of mine recalls a day she walked into an office meeting with her shirt on back to front and a different shoe on each foot. In her hurry to get herself out of the house and two children up, dressed, fed and off to school, she had left the house looking (unknowingly) rather unprofessional!

Is this your life?

6am

Most mornings are a 400metre dash around the house – waking up children and prompting them to get ready (if they are old enough, otherwise you can add getting them ready to your to do list; that is unless hubby obliges - if you have one). Then you have to make breakfast (and squeeze in some tidying up or laundry at the same time) and get yourself ready for work before dashing off to do the school run (often with a piece of toast on your lap as you drive because you haven't had time to eat). Once they are dropped off, you find somewhere to park and jump on the tube to get to work; where once again you are sandwiched between two people, your face in someone's armpit and your leg dangerously close to some stranger's. What an auspicious start to the day! P.s. did somebody say 'quiet time' or better still do you remember what that is?

9am

At your desk, the working day begins and you work conscientiously till 11am, feeling quite smug and on top of things until the phone rings. Dread fills you when you see your child's school number and you groan on answering it when they ask you to pick her up because she's feeling poorly. The school is on the other side of town (near home). You put on your sweetest voice and ask your friend who's a stay at home mum to pick her up and keep an eye on her for you; she kindly agrees and you breathe a sigh of relief.

She gets up earlier to travel into work every day, or spends time every night doing a long list of domestic chores before going to bed...

At lunch time, out come those bills you've been meaning to pay. If you don't do it today, they become overdue and you know you can't afford those overdue charges. In the last 10 minutes you grab a sandwich and have a munch before getting back to work.

4.30pm

You are able to get off work without being asked to do something at the last minute which often delays you till 5.30 or sometimes later. Hubby normally picks up your son but as he's working late today you head off and manage to get to your sons school to pick him up from after school club; then onto pick up your daughter from your

friends house. You put the key in the lock at 6pm, exhausted and ready to flop- but the delights of dinner preparation, laundry sorting, home work supervision and children's bed time routines await you.

8pm

You flop on the sofa, exhausted. At that point, a key turns in the lock and hubby is back. You are too exhausted to get up and greet him and choose instead to wait for him to walk in. He heads straight for the kitchen and you reluctantly get up. You eat and chat together before heading to the sitting room and flick through channels. At 9.30 you are ready to drop and sincerely hope that man has no amorous plans for tonight!

A woman's work

Women still do the majority of the household chores, despite their increased participation in the labour market. Women spend 2 and half hours a day on average on housework (excluding shopping and childcare) [5].

What women do

Household regular
- Weekly grocery shopping
- Cooking-1-3 meals a day (taking an average of 30 minutes for each meal)
- Cleaning- scrubbing, dusting, shining, wiping, vacuuming, bed sheet change etc
- Laundry – putting things in the machine and dryer, sorting and ironing, dropping and picking up dry cleaning.

Childcare
- Take children to school and back daily
- Organise children's activities e.g. holiday and extra curricular activities, parties
- Ferry them to and from those activities.

- Visits to the dentist, optician, barbers/hairdressers, doctors.
- School uniform and clothes shopping (this happens frequently as children grow at an alarming rate).
- Homework supervision.
- Babysitting/entertaining of children
- Attending school meetings - teachers meetings, concerts, miscellaneous events

Household administration
- Banking – Reviewing statements, paying bills and cheques
- Renewals – insurance (car & home), licenses, car tax discs
- Miscellaneous Household repairs

Household miscellaneous
- Bulk Household purchases
- Planning birthdays
- Planning holidays/travel

spouses working full time jobs mean there's often very little time for meaningful interaction. Couples spend on average about 2 and half hours per day on shared activities together[7]. During weekdays shared time averages about 2 hours per day, increasing to about 3 and half hours per day at weekends. Guess what the main shared activity is for couples? Watching television together. Shared time watching television averages almost an hour a day and accounts for about a third of all shared time together. Social activities and entertainment together average about a quarter of an hour per day [7].

The effects of the way we live

Poor health - The Hurried Woman Syndrome (HWS)

With this kind of schedule is it no wonder that we are stressed, often overweight (from eating unhealthy food because we don't have time to prepare nutritious meals) and spiritual featherweights (God is often the easiest to leave out of our schedule because we can't see Him). Such is the pace of our life that career women now have their own disease. An American doctor has coined the term Hurried Woman Syndrome (HWS)[6] to describe an illness caused by chronic stress caused by combining work and family life. The symptoms of this illness include tiredness, increased appetite, lack of motivation, low self esteem, feelings of guilt and weight gain. A survey by Prima magazine in 2005 found that three quarters of women suffer from at least five of the symptoms of HWS. This combination of symptoms can sometimes lead to clinical depression or other serious illnesses.

Strained marriages

It's not only our health that's suffering. The truth is that our marriages are strained because both

The research make's it clear. We are just not investing enough in our marriages. Our careers demand so much of us that we have little left to give each other. Research shows that the more educated a couple are and the more they earn, the less time they spend together[9]. As far back as 1995, it was identified that dual career couples in the United States have the highest rate of divorce[10].

> *...research shows that British parents who work full-time spend just 19 minutes every day "caring (directly) for their own children".*

Poor parenting

Unfortunately, many of our children are also neglected to varying degrees as a result of our working patterns.

By committing to demanding work schedules we have had to delegate the parenting of our children to au-pairs, nannies and after school clubs. The turnover of childcare givers in some households due to the transient nature of childcare arrangements is also unsettling for many young children, who are forced into quite intimate relationships with a variety of adults as a result. Research by Working Mother magazine shows that a third of working mums have sent a sick child to school[11]. I guess they couldn't get the time off work to stay at home and care for the child.

What about our non working hours? Whilst we may spend the evenings with our children, research shows that British parents who work full-time spend just 19 minutes every day "caring (directly) for their own children"[12]. This is only enough time to eat a quick breakfast together or have a couple of bed-time stories. The same source states that a further 16 minutes is spent looking after their children as a "secondary activity", but this means that they are doing something else at the same time. We are also not investing enough educationally in our children as a result. 60 % of British women and 66% of British men do not help their children with homework.[13] At the end of the day, we are just too tired for algebra and Shakespeare!

Ready for something new?

This is a clarion call out to my sisters. I believe that its time for us to take a good look at our schedules and commitments' and ask how we can design a life that is balanced and rich not unbalanced and stressful. Are you ready for the journey? If so, let's find out where you are – take the quiz to find out.

Life balance and well being Survey [14]

Please circle which response is most accurate for you

1. I have a good sense of my emotional, relational, physical and spiritual capacities, intentionally pulling back to rest and fill my "tank" often (Mark 1:21-39).
   a) Very true
   b) Mostly true
   c) Sometimes true
   d) Not true

2. I have time to cook and eat healthy meals and exercise regularly.
   a) Very true
   b) Mostly true
   c) Sometimes true
   d) Not true

3. People who work with me would describe me as a dependable, organised and timely person.
   a) Very true
   b) Mostly true
   c) Sometimes true
   d) Not true

4. I regularly spend time in prayer, bible study and devotional activities (at least 5 days a week).
   a) Very true
   b) Mostly true
   c) Sometimes true
   d) Not true

5. My husband and children (or other key people) get enough time, care and attention from me most of the time.
   a) Very true
   b) Mostly true
   c) Sometimes true
   d) Not true

6. The fruit of the spirit is evident in my life and interactions with others (*patience, longsuffering, self-control, goodness, kindness, faithfulness*).
   a) Very true
   b) Mostly true
   c) Sometimes true
   d) Not true

7.   I do not feel guilty about taking time off to rest, look after myself or to enjoy a hobby or interest.

a)   Very true
b)   Mostly true
c)   Sometimes true
d)   Not true

8.   I do not often feel overwhelmed by the duties, demands and responsibilities of life.

a)   Very true
b)   Mostly true
c)   Sometimes true
d)   Not true

9.   I meet regularly with a small group to share spiritual fellowship.

a)   Very true
b)   Mostly true
c)   Sometimes true
d)   Not true

10.   I make time regularly to spend with friends and extended family whose company I enjoy.

a)   Very true
b)   Mostly true
c)   Sometimes true
d)   Not true

11.   Those close to me would say that I am good at balancing family, rest, work, and play in a biblical way (Ex. 20:8).

a)   Very true
b)   Mostly true
c)   Sometimes true
d)   Not true

12.   I feel at peace with God and 'on track' in my life at this time.

a)   Very true
b)   Mostly true
c)   Sometimes true
d)   Not true

Award yourself

3 points for every a) answer
2 points for every b) answer
1 points for every c) answer
0 points for every d) answer

Life Balance

25-36 You know how to balance the key demands on your life and to give proper attention to various areas. As a result your sense of well being should be strong and your life should be productive and successful on the whole.

Read on to learn a few tips to thrive even more.

13-24 On the whole you are able to balance the key demands on your life, although you do struggle to give proper attention to some areas. As a result your general sense of well being should be good but read on to learn some time management and prioritisation skills that can help you achieve a better life/ work balance.

12 and below You often feel out of kilter and overwhelmed by the various demands on your life and struggle to give proper attention to various areas. As a result your sense of well being is compromised and you may struggle at being productive and successful on the whole.

Read on and take some time to look critically at your various roles and commitments (especially chapters 3-7) and learn some time management and prioritisation skills that can help you achieve a better life/ work balance.

Chapter 2

Are you
thriving or striving?

Strive = an effortful attempt to attain a goal, to strain, to exert much effort or energy
Thrive = to bloom, flourish or prosper; to make steady progress (in a way that is balanced and healthy).

Oftentimes there's a psychology that dictates our pace of, and approach to, life. Yes, modern life is busy; but the pace of our life is often driven by internal and not external factors. A while ago I realised that my life was often busy because I had a million and one things I felt I needed to achieve or accomplish. So many of us have something to prove - we are working towards an ideal day or time when we'll have the 5 bedroom house, huge savings in the bank, a second, third or fourth property, children in the best schools or a certain job title. It is this drive to create the ideal life or 'achieved' life 'someday in the future' that often rubs us of the pleasure of today. These things

drive us and consume chunks of our day to day life, alongside the basic things we need to do to keep bread on the table and a roof over our heads. It's a life full of striving.

we'll have the 5 bedroom house, huge savings in the bank, a second, third or fourth property, children in the best schools or a certain job title.

One of the books I find most interesting in the bible is the book of Ecclesiastes. I find it interesting because it is a book that explores the meaning of life. In it Solomon talks about his quest for significance and meaning in life. First he sought out wisdom; but he found out that wisdom brought sorrow and grief - Ecclesiastes 1:12-17 (because knowledge often imputes responsibility). Then he sought out pleasure – laughter, wine, music and women (or love and relationships) – Ecclesiastes 2:1-3,10a. And you know where that led him – more wives and concubines than you can count and a divided spiritual heart. Then Solomon focused on achievement and acquisition; he undertook great projects. He built houses, planted vineyards, gardens and parks. He had many employees, herds, flocks and gold and made a great name for himself- Ecclesiastes 2:4-9. Much of our lives like Solomon's can be preoccupied with striving-up with the Jones's- Ecclesiastes ..., ... way, did you hear the Jones are in debt from trying to maintain appearances?) or to gain more degrees and knowledge.

On our way to 'there' we trample on the 'now'

We chase these things because we think they'll deliver something to us – significance, happiness, contentment. We steal time from family or devotion to do that evening course to get that qualification or work the extra hours to get that promotion. I believe in impact and achievement but I think we must always count the cost and ask ourselves if it's worth it. What was Solomon's final verdict? At the end of it all, he found his striving 'meaningless and (like) chasing after the wind'- Ecclesiastes 2:17. Throughout the book, the futility of striving after the wind is highlighted. Chasing after that which can never be caught the wind. Significance, I have discovered, comes from a sense of internal value given by God not by achievements. Money can buy fun and comfort but unfortunately it doesn't buy happiness and contentment. Happiness and contentment is a matter of choice, not what is in ones bank account.

The truth is that if we don't manage these internal drivers they can take away from instead of adding to the quality of our lives.

The truth is that if we don't manage these internal drivers they can take away from, instead of adding to the quality of our lives. We can live so much for that idealised day in the future that today is robbed of its value and meaning. I am coming to understand the importance of simple pleasures. Someone said the best things in life are free – an early hour time with God, an unhurried Saturday morning in bed with the children-reading or hanging out, a family meal enjoyed together or a long chat with a good friend. Even if work is hellish and money is tight, finding time to squeeze these simple pleasures in every now and then can infuse elements into our lives that cause us to move from a constant state of striving and to begin to thrive. To abstain from striving doesn't mean that we have no goals or ambitions; rather it means that we give careful thought to what our goals are and that we plan to achieve them in a way that allows us to contribute to and enjoy the other things that are important in life.

After years of exploration, Solomon deduced a few principles for meaningful living

Honour God
'Fear God and keep his commandments, for this is the whole duty of man'
- Ecclesiastes 9:9

Be a blessing to others
I know that there is nothing better for men than to be happy and do good while they live - **Ecclesiastes 12:13**

Enjoy your relationships
'Enjoy life with your wife… - **Ecclesiastes 9:9**

Do work you enjoy
A man can do nothing better than to …. find satisfaction in his work - **Ecclesiastes 2:24**

Enjoy simple pleasures
Then I realized that it is good and proper for a man to man to eat and drink…
- Ecclesiastes 5:18

PART 2

Creating a life that works

Makeover

Chapter 3

LIFE QUESTION 1 - PURPOSE

If you are serious about a life makeover, there are a series of questions you need to ask yourself.

Purpose
What am I here for? What has God created me to do?'

One of the things that made Jesus so effective was that He was a man of purpose. He was very clear about who He was and what He was here to do.

> [42] *Now when it was day, He departed and went into a deserted place. And the crowd sought Him and came to Him, and tried to keep Him from leaving them; 43but He said to them, "I must preach the kingdom of God to the other cities also, because for this purpose I have been sent."*
>
> *Luke 4:42-43*

Many of us women unfortunately lack such clarity. My husband often says 'When there is no purpose, abuse in inevitable'. Because our lives have no clear purpose and demands are many, we strike out in many directions - try our hands at this and that and dabble in this or that; but because we do not give focused attention to anything we make little progress and become stressed.

Also because women's lives are so often wrapped up in the care of others, it's easy to lose ourselves. It's important to ask yourself, 'What am I here for? What has God created me to do?' It can be a hard question to answer and needs to be deduced with much prayer. As women we may also find that our life purpose alters with seasons of life (*see chapter 6 for more on this*); but it may be helpful to start with relational indicators.

Relational indicators

- If you are a Christian, a key life purpose is worshipping God and growing in devotion to Him and in Christ likeness.

- If you are a wife, another life purpose is being a supportive and loving wife to your husband.

- If you are a mother, another life purpose is being attentive and nurturing and bringing up each child to attain his or her full potential.

Many women find that their life purpose is wrapped up in fulfilling their relational roles and are content to do just that. Unfortunately society now disparages women who choose to look after their home and family full time. We no longer value so called traditional values or roles. Raising a family is a high calling.

So special is this role that on a number of occasions God specifically commissions a parent into raising a warrior. Samson's mother (Judges 13:1-7), John the Baptist's father (Luke 1:11-20) and Mary the mother of Jesus (Luke 1:26-38) are examples. And certainly no women should be embarrassed that despite her degree she's a stay at home mum – it's worthy work.

However, some women believe that there is another purpose that God has for them perhaps in the workplace or society and that is also acceptable. Even in bible times the bible records a woman judge/ political leader (Deborah) and the Proverbs 31 woman was a consummate business woman. The important thing is to make time to discern what God's purpose is for you in each season of your life.

Dispelling the myths

Oftentimes when purpose is mentioned, some immediately envisage a spiritual role with a title in the church; or envision some dramatic role revealed in a dramatic way. While some people will receive a revelation of purpose through a dream or vision, this is the exception and not the rule. The reality is that many people stumble almost into their purpose. As they utilize some gift that God has given them, they find themselves in a place of purpose. Queen Esther's beauty made her queen and put her in a position to access power to save a nation. Nehemiah's burden for the walls of Jerusalem made him a nation restorer. Dorcas's sewing gift saw her become a comforter to widows and the dispossessed – Acts 9:39.

Identify your gift/s or talent/s

One of the easiest ways to begin to discover purpose is to identify what you are good or gifted at. Every body has a natural talent, something that they do easily and well or that they excel at. Your gift could be a natural gift or a spiritual gift (see 1 Corinthians 12:7-11, 28) or a learned skill that you excel at or have a natural aptitude for.

identify what you are good or gifted at.

It could be
- writing
- singing
- a flair for art or fashion design
- public speaking or oratory skills
- leadership
- organizational skills
- domestic skills e.g. sewing and cookery
- numeracy
- athletic ability
- comedy/humour
- beauty/elegance
- playing a specific instrument
- diplomacy /people skills

....the list is endless

My talents/gifts (*Think -what do I get commended for the most by friends and colleagues*)

1 ....
2 ....
3 ....

Identify your area of passion

Another key to identifying purpose is discovering an area of passion.

- Do you find yourself particularly moved by a cause?
- Do you have a lot of enthusiasm for something?
- Do you feel especially joyous or fulfilled when doing something?
- Are you burdened with a particular cause?
- Does a particular group of people or sector of society have a pull on you?

- Moses was passionate about the liberty of the Jews in Egypt and was eventually sent by God to deliver that nation.
- The apostle Paul was passionate about making Christ known and traversed most of ancient Europe doing so.
- Dorcas cared about the welfare of widows and on her deathbed her life's work to them was evidenced.

- David delighted in worship and became known as the man after God's heart.

Our passion is an indicator of our area of calling or that which we are called to. If something – a cause, a group of people, an arena - draws us time and again; we should give some thought to it and ask what God may be saying to us through this desire or 'pull'.

My passions

1 ....

2 ....

3 ....

Positional advantages

Many times we enter into life purpose when the combination of our gift, passion and positional advantages and circumstance's create an opportunity to act. Nehemiah entered into purpose when his gift (leadership and administration) and his passion for Jerusalem and his positional advantage as the king's cupbearer enabled him to act in a season when His nation had a great need that he could meet. He was able to leverage his relationship with the king to make a real difference to that nation. So ask yourself - what positional advantages enable you to access power or resources to be a blessing to others?

Positional advantages can be as a result of your

- An office/achievements- that give you standing with people
- Line of work – perhaps you have contacts, resources or knowhow in a particular area that God could use to really impact others for good.
- Status – your standing in society
- Connections – those you have access to
- Background – things or people you have experienced in the past that can be of use to a set of people for example.

Positional advantages I have

1 ....

2 ....

3 ....

Look at the opportunities possible because of that position and ask if God desires you to leverage that position and your gift and passion's to make a real difference.

Prayerfully ask God to help you discern His purpose for your life in every situation and with every opportunity.

A few years ago Funke Adeaga stepped out and decided to make a living from her passion. Read on to find out how she used a gift of design as a platform for a career makeover.

Making a living out of your passion

'...I have always had a flair for design and love combining colours to create innovative looks and styles'

As far as I can recall, I never consciously embarked on a career in fashion. As is often the case in life, events take place which propel one towards a path that was not consciously chosen.

I was trained as a lawyer and had already begun a career in the mortgage Industry. However life took an unexpected turn when I was suddenly made redundant. This presented an opportunity for me to think carefully about my future and to reach the decision to explore what had always been little more than a passionate pastime. At the time I knew that I had this interest, other people constantly told me that it was a gift. I also knew that it gave me joy and that my job at the time was just that and whilst it paid well and held the possibility of advancement, it did not give me lasting fulfilment.

I have always had a flair for design and love combining colours to create innovative

looks and styles. I also love shirts and tailored trouser suits and I wanted to create a look for women that was functional, yet stylish and feminine. I felt that there was a gap in the market with regards to women's shirts that combine three specific features: bold designs, colour and style. In the four years since JSapphirah was birthed, we have evolved to where we are presently: our signature style is our bold and unfettered combination of bright patterns and prints.

> ...*our signature style is our bold and unfettered combination of bright patterns and prints.*

was a dream and turn it into reality. Thankfully, I have a very supportive husband who has been a tremendous source of encouragement over the years.

Overcoming self doubt to reach for your dreams

The initial challenge was in overcoming self doubt and having the courage to take what

It was not easy; however I felt strongly that it was a risk I had to take. I prayed a lot about it and felt the Lord leading me in the self-employment direction. My redundancy was timely and although in the end the career shift was not an easy decision, it made it less traumatic somehow. The initial start up funding was from my redundancy pay package and then subsequently from our family savings. With hindsight I have seen God's guidance from the beginning - I was inexperienced, without previous training and with modest finances. The possibility for failure was high, but God has been faithful. God has led me (*and still leads me*) to the right people at the right time, has opened diverse and unusual doors of opportunities and encouraged me in amazing ways when I have needed it most. I could never have embarked on this venture without the assurance that it was His will for my life.

Maintaining the passion

Most times we want to have a perfect environment before we start a business, however I believe things would never be 100% perfect. The most important thing is to be passionate about what you want to do; it should be something that you would do even if you were not paid for it. Also you need unwavering commitment for the business, diligence, focus and it is important not to try to do too many things at the same time and explore different avenues for funding. I believe in our product completely; I am very passionate about what I do and feel very privileged to be doing something that I love so much. It is a thrill to see the business evolve day by day and I look forward to the future with great excitement.

Being a business owner means I can create time for other things that are important to me

I am actively involved at my church where I presently oversee the women's ministry as well as the customer facing departments. I also run a mentoring programme for young ladies as part of the women's ministry and serve as Editor of Adivah, our magazine for women.

Funke's time/life management tips for women

- I have learnt that people will value your time if you show them first that you value your time.

- Focus on the things that are high priority, do not try to do too many things at the same time. If you try to do too many things at the same time you will find out that each task is half complete.

- Postpone low priority tasks.

- In life there will always be distractions, learn to recognise the distractions in your life and block them out.

- Motivate yourself.

- Stay organised especially as a business person.
    - Get files, and learn to file documents away as soon as you get them and have read them.
    - Put reminders on your phone and PDA to keep you on top of things.

- Always look on the bright side of life and find something to be thankful for.

From dentist to performance poet -meet Jumi Fola-alade as she shares her journey to discover and live her passion and gift.

'......I have always loved words and had flair with words and longed to work with words everyday as opposed to occasionally. I love writing (it transports me to another realm!)'

Discovering and using my gift

I changed career track because I felt that I was living someone else's dream, acting out a script that wasn't mine. I had a real hunger to meet a deeper more urgent and personal need: to achieve inner excellence. I have always loved words and had flair with words and longed to work with words everyday as opposed to occasionally.

> *I had a real hunger to meet a deeper more urgent and personal need: to achieve inner excellence.*

I love writing (*it transports me to another realm*) I am so blessed now to be able to reveal aspects of God through my poetry and to challenge people into more intimate relationships with Him through it.

Overcoming my fears and stepping out

My main apprehension in changing career track was to do with the sustainability of my interest in this career path and if I would find a continual challenge to engage my adventurous, free and creative spirit. The other concern was one I think what we all feel when our pounding hearts bring us to a road less travelled.

We may not have been 'trained' to travel that road and we find no footprints ahead to show us the way.

Taking the step to move from job to working your passion

Pray and wait until the One who responds is the One who made you and then and then alone run with His counsel. Assuredly there will be many well-meaning voices, but His voice will remain audible above the noise of the thunders of the storms that will rage at various points along that new path.

> *I deeply appreciate the fact that I can be creatively engaged with work that absolutely inspires me...*

The benefits of a flexible work-life utilising my passion

I deeply appreciate the fact that I can be creatively engaged with work that absolutely inspires me, generates a decent enough income and most of all gives me a life. And because I am able to work from home, I don't lose out much on being around the children and that is deeply satisfying to me. I am also able to be very involved in the children's school (*I am the Chair of the PTA*), my local church and women's empowerment groups.

Life/time management tips for other women

Understand that life is finite. I like John Ortberg's reference to the empty glass jars our lives are presented as, which will end up being filled with all kinds of stuff. I believe true success comes when first things are put first into the jar of life. Imagine these four priorities as the balls that the jar was made to carry: God, People, The Call and Joy. Once the things that matter most are in place, all else, all many obligations are just like sand that can fill up the empty spaces in the Jar of Life. But many of us have things the other way round – we are fragile glass jars brimming with sand, trying to squeeze in what should be our main priorities.

LIFE
QUESTION 2&3 - PRIORITIES AND PRINCIPLES

Priorities
What are my priorities?

The Cambridge dictionary defines priority as 'something that is very important and must be dealt with before other things'.

Once you have determined your purpose (and I understand that this can be a herculean task, so give yourself time), it should be easy to deduce what your priorities are. It's important to ask yourself what the most important, meaningful or valuable things in your life are. Is it career advancement, spending time with or nurturing your children, your marriage, your health or your spiritual life?

List what you feel are the most important priorities in your life at this time in order of importance.

1 ....

2 ....

3 ....

4 ....

5 ....

Once you have done this, have a quick think about your comittments and how much time is presently allocated to each priority. Do not be surprised if like many people find that you are spending more time on the less important things.

Priority 1 / Average Time Spent ....

Priority 2 / Average Time Spent ....

Priority 3 / Average Time Spent ....

Priority 4 / Average Time Spent ....

Priority 5 / Average Time Spent ....

Do not be surprised if like many people you find that you are spending more time on the less important things. We do have to work to make a living, but if our work is causing us to neglect the more important things in our life, its time to ask ourselves some important questions. As it's commonly said, no one ever says on their bed death, 'Bring me those unfinished work files, I want to see what work I can complete before I cross over to the other side'. Rather on that momentous occasion, we want to be surrounded by the ones we love so that we can let them know how much they mean to us. Unfortunately, many have regrets on that day because they realise they invested in things instead of people and they have run out of time to

> *'...it's also important to ask yourself what should be your priority at particular stages of your life'*

love. It's important, before it's too late, to make sure that our lives are invested in the most meaningful things.

Aside of what you think is a priority, it's also important to ask yourself what should be your priority at particular stages of your life. If you have small children, a special needs child or parents who need care for example; it is important to

give some thought to your role in their lives in that season of their and your life. Children grow up and leave home, sometimes earlier than you anticipated.

'...it's also important to ask yourself what should be your priority at particular stages of your life'.

We are currently mooting the idea of one of our children attending boarding school in a few years time. It suddenly

occurred to me that if we decide that he should go, I won't see him everyday as I do currently for weeks or perhaps months at a time. Your children wont always be around; so while they are still young and with you- it should be a priority to nurture and care for them to the best of your ability.

The myth of quality time

One of our priorities should be time with our family. Don't believe the myth of quality time. After a long days work we simply don't have quality to give. Quality time to a child is quantity time. I've found that quality time comes out of quantity time. You can't schedule a baby's first steps or words. You can't say to your teenager, 'I am giving you 10 minutes of quality time, now tell me all your problems'.

Rather it's when we take the time to be with our children - over a leisurely meal or walk or whilst driving to a family outing that issues of their heart come pouring out and bonding and intimacy takes place. I've had to spend hours at times prying out information from my children about specific issues. Parenting takes time; you can't always fit it in between a high powered lunch and business meeting. I believe its time to ask ourselves some serious questions about how we are raising the next generation.

Other important priorities that require quantity time is our spiritual and physical wellbeing.

Many times our wrong use of time can be due to esteem issues (which drive us to spend time proving things to ourselves or others)

I have discovered that we need chunks of unhurried time to live effective spiritual lives — to be still, to pray, to rest in God. And maintaining the body in optimum condition also requires investment of time in research, working out and cooking nutritious meals. Time we simply don't have on our current schedules.

Think long term

Many of our priorities are also out of place because we think in the short term. Very few people have taken the time to think long term about their life.

It's important for example to think about how long we want to work and where we want to be in 5, 10 or 20 years. And give some thought to when you'd like to retire and how much we'll need to do so. Many are simply too busy working to take the time to think about the future.

Also ask yourself, aside of work achievements, when I look back on my life, what kind of things do I want to see in other areas of my life. What kind of marriage do you want to have? Don't just say a good one. What would you like to be the main characteristic of your marriage? If you could choose one word

to describe your ideal marriage what would it be - nurturing, intimate, fun, or supportive for example? Then ask yourself what kind of adults do I want my children to be and what do I need to do now to help them become that? Last but not least, what kind of relationship do I want to have with God and what do I need to do to make that a reality?

Perhaps the most important reason for thinking long term about our lives is that it can help us to quickly determine what should be priority now. It forces us to confront whether how we live now will get us where we want to be in the future. Or it causes's us to weigh the long term value or importance of our daily activities.

Chapter 4

What do I want my life to look like in 5, 10 or 20 Years

My work life

My marriage

My children (the fruit of me raising them)

My walk with God

Esteem and Values

Many times our wrong use of time can be due to esteem issues (which drive us to spend time proving things to ourselves or others) or value issues (about what is important in life). Read on below where I explore this issue alongside the issue of spiritual leadings.

Spiritual leadings

Last but not least in this section, what is God telling you your priority is at this time in your life? Oftentimes Gods agenda and ours can be very different. I remember as a newly wed being hell-bent (literally) on getting my legal career off the ground (for which I had studied 4 courses in 2 continents over 7years for). 6 months into marriage, I was pregnant but remained undeterred in my dream to be a legal eagle. I prepared to drop and run (give birth and go back to work immediately). My efforts to find work at the level I was looking for were unfruitful but I remained steadfast in my desire and hope. I wasn't listening – to my time of life or the quiet whispers of the Spirit.

The penny dropped about a year after I gave birth as I tried to prepare a talk for some students I had been invited to address. I just couldn't get a handle on the message and as I drove through the city and nearer to the address, panic set in as I had nothing prepared to say to them. In desperation, I cried 'God, what do I say to these people?' A few minutes later a thought came to my mind – I realised I was driving through the City of London, the financial centre of the nation and a place of aspiration for work for many of the students I would be addressing. Immediately I knew what to say to them.

I knew that like me at that time, they had probably mixed up work and identity. They desired big titles and work in certain sectors so that they could feel valuable or that they had arrived. Whilst I am all for doing one's best and doing well, we are mistaken if we think our salary or our job title is what makes us significant. Many of us are working crazy hours for titles and money.

On that drive I realised that God was asking me to look at my values and esteem system.

On that drive I realised that God was asking me to look at my values and esteem system. Could I be happy and content if I never got a job in the City and would I still feel my life had counted if I never worked as a lawyer? Those things are important on this side, but I needed to ask myself if my worth and value depended on what I did or who I am in God? It may be a question you

need to ask yourself too; because once I had answered it, working in the City and earning a six figure salary was no longer my life ambition. My priorities became clearer. Take some time once again to think about what your priorities should be in this season, and long term.

Principles

What principles will guide my life?

The Cambridge dictionary defines a guiding principle as 'an idea which influences you very much when making a decision or considering a matter'.

It is important if you are serious about a life make over that you decide what your guiding principles and life motivators will be. Or once you have determined your life priorities then it is important that you distill some rules or guide for living as a result of that. For example if one of my priorities is my children, then one of the guiding principles of my life will be not taking on work that means I will have very little time with them.

If one of my priorities is my health, then my guiding principle is to make choices that continuously promote my health and well being. If one of my priorities is a closer spiritual walk with God, then one of my guiding principles will be to live my life in a way that facilitates such a relationship. Think about and jot down what guiding principles you will apply to honor the priorities you have identified.

Guiding principles for my life

1 ....

2 ....

3 ....

4 ....

5 ....

Chapter 5

LIFE
QUESTION 4 – CHOICES

What choices do I need to make?

Once you have determined your priorities and formulated guiding principles for each one; it is important to decide what changes you are willing to make to ensure that your use of time and your priorities align. This is where the rubber meets the road and where many women shrink back. For years I knew I needed to make some important decisions but I shrank back – I enjoyed my work, we needed the finances, what would happen if I left my role? All these questions kept me from making necessary changes for a long while.

Unfortunately many women are pushed to the brink before they make necessary life changes. I remember a dear lady who was confronted with the fact that her 12 year old could barely read. She had been too busy at work and with church activities to notice that her daughter was lagging behind educationally. This discovery was the wake up call that forced her to change her schedule and drop various commitments so she would have more time to devote to her daughter.

Many women may benefit from looking at their work schedule and career commitments. The 9-5 can be a grind if you have family commitments that mean you are constantly pulled between the two worlds. It may be time to look at the work options open to you that will allow you to devote more time to the family if that is important to you.

She had been too busy at work and with church activities to notice that her daughter was lagging behind educationally.

Below we meet three women who designed their work schedule around their family life.

Going Part Time

Meet Biyi. She is a married woman in her early 40's with two children. In this article she talks about her decision to stop full time work and the benefits for her family life as a result.

I started work as a generalist HR Advisor. I worked fulltime for full time for over 10years. When I had my daughter life was very stressful for me and my husband. I was climbing up the career ladder and had started working at management level within Human resources.

Another huge benefit of working part time is that it has given me time to invest in relationships.

I was very busy at work and was stressed by it mentally as I always brought my work home with me (i.e. mentally). Me and my husband became burnt out and had no quality time together as a couple or as a family. We would both get home in the evening tense and irritable and we struggled to cook nutritious meals after a long days work; even when we did we were often too tired to enjoy them. The housework became burdensome and everything was such a chore.

The conclusive analysis of the situation was that things were not working properly and we could not go on like that.

We decided that I would work part-time so that we could have a better quality of life as a family. I feel fortunate that my husband and I are clear on the priorities we have with regards to our children and our expectations for family life. Working part time does have an impact on your finances as there is not the same amount of money coming in as one is used to from full time work.

But I got used to the change after a few months. I learnt to prioritise and cut out what is not really necessary. There are also a lot of things you don't have to spend money on that you would if you were working full time e.g. not having to pay for lunch is a big saver.

As a part timer one has more time to hunt out better deals on items of clothing and other things. There is also time to buy natural ingredients and make more nutritious meals which are cheaper than processed convenience food we buy because we don't have time to cook. One may even save money on childcare as well because there is no need to pay for afterschool care which you would have to if working fulltime so overall it may actually be more cost effective to work part time.

A woman considering going part time also has to be realistic about its implications for her career prospects. Even though Human Resources as a profession lends itself to part-time working, when you are working part time its hard to participate in after work social activities, which are an essential part of work life. I try and socialise with work colleagues during lunch to make up but it's easy to get excluded. Working part time can also restrict promotion opportunities, but you've got to decide if you want a high powered job or a close relationship with your family.

The other day I was taking my daughter to school

and she said to me 'Mum, when are you going to get a nice jeep like all the other mums in my school?' I told her that I could get one but I would have to work full time to pay for it and would be so busy working that somebody else would have to take her to and from school and stay with her until I got back from work. She looked at me and said 'Ok mum I get the message. It's ok".

The benefits of working part time far outweigh the cost for me. I find that that even though there is always some kind of stressor at any point in my

> *the children and I are not stressed and we can spend quality time together as a family...*

life, it is easier to manage because I don't have a full work schedule. I don't have to negotiate after school activities, homework or shopping with my employer or husband. Another huge benefit of working part time is that it has given me time to invest in relationships. I have time to drop and pick up my daughter from school. This has proved very important as I am able to gain valuable information from my daughter whilst doing the school run and find out what her issues are.

Working part time has also been very beneficial for my marriage. When I was working full time I would pick my daughter up from school after work, get home at about 6.45pm and then try to get dinner ready, get her to bed and everything else prepared for the next day. It was so stressful. At about 10pm the grumpiness would set in and there was no time to have a decent relationship or quality time with my husband. Nowadays when my husband walks in after work, his dinner is ready and there is peace in the house; the children and I are not stressed and we can spend quality time together as a family and have couple time when they go to bed.

Working part time has enabled me to have quite a balanced life. People close to me feel that I have the best of both worlds. I am happy enough at the moment as I am able to juggle things quite realistically and do not get overburdened with things. I have a good fit for my family as I am there for my children and husband, I can participate in chosen church activities and I do work that I find interesting and enjoyable.

Biyi's life management tips for women

- Do what works for you
- Make sure you and your spouse agree on your choices
- Keep your options open
- Make sure you enjoy a

balanced life by having some time for yourself
- And finally.............take time to understand the seasons in your life and enjoy them. Young marriages grow old, young children grow up and the only constant in life is change so make sure in the scheme of things you keep on top of something that you enjoy (be it a hobby / interest or sphere of work) so that as and when the seasons of life change you will always have something that keeps you happy!!

Job share/partnership
Kenny is a lawyer, she runs a law firm in Central London with a friend

I am a lawyer and decided to start a law firm with another woman some years ago. Being in partnership has meant that I can be my own boss yet share my job which is a great thing. Because we are both women we understand and are highly supportive of each other. We planned having our children around each other and took it in turns so literally I would be pregnant, give birth and once I was on maternity leave she would get pregnant.

Once I returned to work after maternity leave it would be time for her to give birth and take maternity leave. We've managed to have 5 perfectly synchronised children between the two of us. Also because I am my own boss (although that has its pressures) I can take time out when necessary to attend my children's school events and suchlike which is very important to me.

We have designed our firm to be family friendly, we don't open till 9.30am so I am able to walk my children to school every day which I really enjoy. All in all I feel very blessed to have been able to organise my work life in a way that honours my family life and for me choosing to work in a partnership is key to that.

Kenny's life management tips for women
- Don't sweat the small stuff.
- Don't try to do it all at once. Instead let different things have priority at different times. There will be times when you know you have to give attention to your children, and there are times when the business will be at the forefront.
- Start your working day with prayer at your desk.

Working from home
Pamela Orji, is a single mum and runs her own business from home.

I run a company called 'Mums with Tots' (www.mumswithtots.com) that promotes the wellbeing of families by providing education and training in first aid skills, and creative development through music and dance for children 0-5 yrs.

I am also in the process of launching a natural skincare range for mothers and babies. Operating a home based business is great because it affords me the flexibility to be able to do what I love and be able to spend time with my daughter in her crucial formative years. More importantly, I get to set my own work hours. I try to keep the bulk of my working hours between 9.30am to 2.30pm when my daughter is at school, though I will often catch up with work emails for about an hour after she goes to bed at 8pm.

You don't need a big budget to start a business; my budget was really small. My initial outlay was about £2000 - my biggest cost at the time was my website, which cost £850 and I started by running Pilates classes in a rented hall.

Whilst I encourage women to start a business if they have a good business idea, its important to note that as

> *...it affords me the flexibility to be able to do what I love and be able to spend time with my daughter ...*

a business owner, you have to keep your vision and passion for the business at the forefront of your mind, especially when times are tough financially, as other people might be depending on you for their livelihood, particularly if you employ people.

Pam's life management tips for women

- Take a few minutes to plan and organise your day so you can be effective.

- Rather than trying to do too much, focus on what is really important and do it well.

- I love the serenity prayer "God grant me the serenity to accept the things I cannot change, the courage to change the things I can and the wisdom to know the difference".

Little changes

You can decide to make a radical change to your working life like some of the women featured here, but some small life changes can make a big difference. Some simple things like

- Rising an hour early to pray or work out.

- Creating a date night once a week so that you can have uninterrupted time with your spouse

- Choosing to turn off the TV for an hour each evening and have a family meal in that time.

- Being intentional about cutting down on after work socialising so you can be home early to spend time with the family.

Choices I am making to use more of my time on my priorities

1

2

3

4

5

Before we look at the last two life questions in chapter 7 we will be exploring the importance of boundaries and working with life seasons in chapter 6.

Chapter 6

BOUNDARIES AND SEASONS

Are you doing too much?

For years I struggled as I tried to keep all the plates' spinning- trying to balance my work with church commitments, personal devotion and family life. I always felt it was a matter of planning – if I managed my time better, if I planned better, I would be able to do everything. I have only recently come to realise that I can't do everything. Have you ever tried to fit a king size duvet into a single duvet cover? It just doesn't work. It may go in, but it looks crumpled and it certainly won't spread over a king size bed in that cover. That's how many of our lives are - we are trying to cram far too much in and our lives are crumpled as a result!

Be selective

Some women have a tendency to say yes to everything. We don't like letting people down and some of us have a martyr complex – we feel we should lay down our lives for everyone.
Once you have identified your priorities, give some thought before you say yes to something that will make a regular demand on your time. Ask yourself

-        Do I have time for this?
-        Is this in line with my priorities?
-        Will this allow me to continue to honour my priorities?

It's important to do this otherwise you will be spending your time on other people's priorities and not yours.

The gift of limits

Perhaps the greatest gift you can give yourself is the gift of limits and boundaries. The Chinese have a proverb – 'If you do this, then you can't do that'. We should realise that every time we say yes to something, it means we say no to something else; every commitment we make means there are other things that we will be unable to commit to.

I know we can do all things through Christ who strengthens us – Philippians 4:13; but we aren't called to do all things. Jesus was selective about his commitments and He didn't let people push Him into roles He wasn't ready for. Expand

I am not superwoman and I am not called to save the world and do all things. The key as we talked about in the last chapter is to isolate our priorities and focus on them. The mistake we make is to think we can do our priorities and everything else. We can't. That's why we need priorities; otherwise less important things will take up our time and we don't want that if we are to be effective. Time is limited so it must be apportioned and you will often find that once you attend to priority items, there is little or no

every time. On the other hand we have saved a lot on child care bills and of course how do you place monetary value on the time spent raising the kids and building the type of home life we desire?

I understand that if one is very career-minded it a tough decision. For me it's been a sacrifice well worth it. The gratification one gets from making a sale, meeting targets or getting a promotion or a pay rise is not there. However I get as much joy and gratification with each smile or hug I get and every "thank you mummy" that comes my way. When I stopped working, I went through a whole process of re-evaluating who I was and what defined me. I felt like some things that I had prided myself in had been stripped away and I had to rediscover who I was outside of all of that. I learnt and I'm still learning to depend on God as I desperately need His strength to be made perfect in my weakness.

I have three kids and I try to have one-on-one time with each child regularly ...

All things considered, I wouldn't go back to a full time office based job now. I have been able to raise my kids myself and to experience or witness most of their special moments. We are a close knit family and the kids feel quite free to really talk about their feelings and concerns and I am better able to keep an eye on what they spend their time doing. Being around the kids most of the time has meant that I have been there to answer most of the questions they have asked about life. Some are trivial but many have been profound and I have at those times been deeply grateful to God that I have been given the opportunity to be there to help mould the way my children view life. I have three kids and I try to have one-on-one time with each child regularly, a special time to talk about whatever they want

to talk about or simply to cuddle, trade stories... what a privilege!

Being a stay at home mum also means that I also am more available to my husband, family and friends. When I feel the kids or my husband or our family life or even my commitments outside of the home need more attention, I can juggle things around to make time for them because my time is somewhat flexible. For instance If I find that my husband and I have been quite busy and have not spent much time together like we'd love to then that goes right to the top of my list and I create time. I love being able to devote my time to the most important people in my life.

Efe's time/life management tips for women

I guess most women think life is a breeze for stay-at-home mums. My experience says otherwise! Self-discipline (not giving in to the lure of daytime TV, munching on everything in sight or hours of aimless window shopping) and time management skills are essential. Keeping a diary really helps. It doesn't matter if it's electronic or a paper diary. Learn to keep and review your to-do lists. Keep a note of successes and challenges, prayer points and praise reports as you go along. Remember, having the type of family life you desire doesn't just happen - you have got to be purposeful in building it. Also, never forget to take time out to relax and recharge.

Now let's have a look at how we can plan and structure our lives practically in the next chapter.

Chapter 7

LIFE QUESTION 5 & 6
PLANS AND STRUCTURES (ORGANISE FOR LIFE)

Plans

What plans must I put in place to makeover my life?

Once you have made choices about life changes to effect your life makeover, you need a plan to make it a reality. You may have decided to work differently for example but that cannot take effect immediately, you need to plan for it. The first step obviously would be to decide how you want to work in the future, and then you may need to plan to speak to your employers about altering your work schedule. Keep together, do not separate as in current design You also need to give some thought to how to respond if they are unable to accommodate the changes you require and your alternatives- perhaps doing research on organisations that allow the working patterns you desire. You might also want to give yourself some transition time to effect the changes e.g. 6-12 months.

Steps to take to effect my life makeover

1

2

3

4

5

Structures

What structures must I put in place daily to make my life work?

The last step in the life makeover process is to determine how to structure your life on a daily basis in order to effect a life makeover with appropriate boundaries and in a way that honors your season of life.

Be an early riser

One way to stay on top of your game is to be an early riser. The early bird, they say, catches the best worm. An extra hour or two gained in the morning can make a big difference and give you a head start so that you don't have to spend the rest of the day playing catch up.

Use that time to

- Pray
- Reflect and review your life
- Plan your day
- Prepare a good breakfast or dinner so your evening is less hectic
- Shop for groceries online
- Catch up with a little housework
- Finish off a work report or document

If you are going to be an early riser, remember that the next day begins the evening before. You must get to bed at a decent hour if you are going to wake up early (say 10pm for a 5pm rise). Women often stay up late catching up on housework and then end up getting up late the next day which puts the whole day in a tailspin. Recognise your limits and be disciplined. Have a deadline for finishing household tasks (say 9pm) and stick to it. You can always finish things up the next morning.

Organise your space

One of the keys to being fruitful is being organised. When you are organised, you create an atmosphere for productivity. You are able to access things you need speedily and there is an ordered environment conducive for work rest or play, On the other hand, disorganisation brings loss- time is wasted looking for things, and the untidy environment cramps creativity. In your home and at work, there should be a space for everything and everything should have its place.

- Create files and folders for important documents, files and papers.
- Label everything so that you don't waste time opening various folders to locate one document.
- Put up shelving and bookcases so that things are easily accessible when needed.
- As much as possible keep clutter at bay. Keep your work desk especially clear of junk.
- Get a memo board to keep record of important upcoming events and for children's school and church bulletins.
- Have regular spring-cleaning every 6 months and throw away stuff that is unused, unwanted or broken.

Schedule your time

Take your time seriously and allocate or schedule your time. I often ask at seminars how many women use a diary or a planner and I am often amazed how few do – that's crazy. If you value your life, start planning your life.

> *One of the keys to being fruitful is being organised. When you are organised, you create an atmosphere for productivity.*

Planning tips

When planning the key as Stephen Covey say's is to put the big rocks (i.e. the most important things) in first. That is, when you schedule put your priorities in first.

- **Plan your year**
  - In addition to a weekly or daily schedule planner, your diary or planner should have a year planner. Your year planner allows you to note and view your year's commitments at a glance.

  - At the beginning of each year before you take on any engagements - mark out birthdays of family members, holiday times, key children's school events such as prize giving, concerts and such like and schedule spiritual retreats (at least once every 3-6 months). Do not take engagements that will mean you can't honour those priorities on that day.

- **Plan your month, your week and your day**
  - At the beginning of each month check your year planner for your commitment's that month and put them into your weekly schedule for the month ahead.

  - Make sure each month that you schedule recreation time, times of rest, couple time with your spouse, an outing with the children, church events you will attend and time for self development - reading, studying, and short courses.

- **Plan your week**
  - On the Monday of each week review the coming week and slot in any new appointments.

- **Plan your day**
  - There should be a game plan for each day. Get a diary with time slots so that each day you can spend 10-15 minutes at the beginning of each day allotting time slots to your priorities and tasks for that day.

  - Put everything down on your schedule- your devotional time, school run schedule and after school activities, preparation and meal time and any home management tasks you have as well as work hours and meetings. You may find it helpful to put your home related stuff in one colour and your work related stuff in another colour.

  - One tip to make life a little less hectic- don't schedule appointments back to back. If possible leave 15-30 minute breaks between appointments so that you don't always feel rushed.

Last but not least - work your schedule. Don't make a schedule and then ignore it or allow other people to overturn it by saying yes to unscheduled things unless it's urgent and you are the only one who can deal with it or you sense it's a divine appointment. Also leave a little space in your schedule for the unexpected, an unallocated hour here or there never killed anyone.

Make time for fun

Last but not least, schedule fun times! Put a treat

in every couple of weeks to give you something to look forward to. It could be an evening soaking in the bath with scented oils and a good book or a lunch date with a friend or a home movie with your hubby. All these things bring refreshing and revitalisation and keep us going.

Create more time
Get hubby in on the act

Despite the advance of women in the marketplace, many men still see housework as the preserve of women and feel when they do it that they are helping out instead of doing their bit. Whilst research shows that men are spending more time with the children, they tend to use that time doing fun things like outings instead of the more mundane day to day tasks of child rearing[8].

Many men simply don't understand what it takes to run a household. Sit your husband down and let him know. Also let him know your burdens, challenges and stresses regarding managing the home and work and how it impacts your marriage. If you are too tired at the end of the day to spend time with him or make love, let him know why. If you have any resentment about carrying the majority of the workload even though you both work tell him so. According to the British Association of Anger Management (BAAM) 16 per cent of women blame housework as the most common cause of arguments with their partner.

Once you have taken the time to express yourself and to hear his thoughts; then explore how you can make things better. Be realistic, some men's work schedule simply doesn't allow them to make significant contributions to the domestic aspects of family life. I know women whose husbands work outside town the whole week and come home for weekends or whose work involves regular travel or is highly demanding in other aspects. Such men simply don't have time for housework on a daily or regular basis.

If you desire him to be more involved at home nonetheless then you must both look at his job schedule critically and ask what changes he is willing to make to facilitate that. Wisdom is required and the better option may be for the women if she has a less lucrative or demanding job to continue to manage the home front for that season o ask him to pay for a cleaner or nanny to lighten the load. It's not politically correct to say that but those are often the responses that marriage and family life require.

> *Sit your husband down and let him know. Also let him know your burdens, challenges and stresses regarding managing the home and work...*

Nevertheless many of us can still get husbands to play a more active role domestically. Be willing for things to be done at a standard lower than you might do it and be careful to request not demand things. To get the ball rolling, its helpful if you state clearly and simply what you expect from him and how he could be more involved around the house. Check out some examples below.

- Ask him what household chores he feels most comfortable doing and then agree some times when he will do that.

- If he balks at housework encourage him to start with bathing children, and overseeing their homework and bedtime routines so that you can use that time for other things.

- Most men can cook at least one dish, you could request he cooks this dish one evening a week so that you have one evening a week that you don't cook.

- Negotiate with him about doing the school run a couple of times a week if his work hours allow it.

- Ask him to do the weekly grocery shop (make sure you send him off with a detailed shopping list)!

- Some men are also happy to do drop offs -dropping off and picking up dry-cleaning, posting mail and suchlike.

- Negotiate a daddy's day – one day a week when he is solely responsible for the children – their getting up and bedtime routines, their feeding, the school run (if his work schedule allows it) and after school activities if it's a week day. Daddy's day is your day off!

Get your kids in on the act

Your children can also help out. From about 8 or 10 years they can begin to have minor household responsibilities. It might be simple things like loading or sorting laundry, tidying their room or overseeing a younger sibling's homework. As they get older (14 or 16) they can cook meals, do some ironing or other household task. Getting boys involved in housework is especially important to help out the next generation of women.

Buy help

It goes without saying that if you can buy help, it helps!
I know a highly successful career woman who is a wife and mother who admits she simply couldn't have done it without the help of her live in nanny / house keeper. Many women cannot afford a fulltime live in nanny but having a cleaner who gives the house a thorough once over once a week is a Godsend and in reach of more people. Check out some options below.

- A full or part time nanny.
- A full or part time housekeeper.
- An au-pair or child minder.
- A cleaner who does a few hours a week.
- Outsourcing ironing.
- A professional caterer you can call on once in a while for home cooked meals.
- A baby sitting or crèche facility you can call on from time to time.

PART 3

Learning to Exhale

Makeover

Chapter 8

SOW
TO THE SPIRIT

An important part of a life makeover that is not merely organisational but transformational is also giving your spirit a makeover. Your spirit is the inner man or person, the unseen part of you that can relate with and commune with God without words. God is a spirit and those who worship him must do so 'in spirit'- John 4:24.

To sow to the spirit is to make time for God, to create times of fellowship, connection and intimacy with God.

Make time for
Prayer
The spirit needs prayer – it craves it.

Many find prayer hard, I have too at times; but prayer is easier when I set time aside for it and I create an environment that encourages it. Rise early or stay up late, find a quiet spot and tell God what's on your heart. Take time also to imagine what could be on His heart and pray about that too. Use drive time and downtimes waiting for the kids to come out of football, swimming or ballet lessons to offer up a few short ones too. Join a prayer group or meet with a prayer partner once a week for intense prayer. Make talking with God part of your daily life.

Worship
The spirit desires to rejoice.

A Christ controlled spirit is a grateful spirit. God doesn't desire a sonorous voice but He does desire true worshippers- John 4:23. Make worship a part of your life. Lift up hands, dance, say thanks, sing – let all of who you are give God glory.

Study
The spirit needs instruction.

Bible study makes God real, accessible and understandable. I am awed time and again when I read the gospels and catch a glimpse at the heart of God reflected in Jesus.

- His wisdom when he said 'Let the one who is without sin cast the first stone'- John 8:7
- His mercy when he said 'Go and sin no more'- John 8:11.
- His power over the elements when he walked on water – John 6:19
- His magnanimity when He restored his captors ear that had been sliced of by a zealous disciple –Luke 22:51

- His thoughtfulness while hung up on the cross, when He turned to John and said 'Woman, behold your son' - John 19:26

Find the time to sit in the word and feast on the word. Move beyond ritual speed reading of 1 chapter a day and take an hour or two on a Saturday morning to begin a topical or word or character study. Stop for a moment or two and offer up a prayer of gratitude over an insight or enter into a bible scene in your mind and really experience the word. Let it come alive for you.

> *To sow to the spirit is to make time for God, to create times of fellowship, connection and intimacy with God.*

Journal
The spirit needs expression.

It is said that reading makes a broad man, but writing makes a specific man.
I have found journaling to be a life saver. It's been an avenue of

- enquiry about life issues
- reflection on happenings around me and the word of God
- recording my life and what God says to me and does in my life
- exploring options
- expressing the deepest issues and concerns of my heart
- praying to God

It's easy to do, get a notebook and just write.

Write about your
- Thoughts
- Questions about life
- Feelings
- Fears or anxieties
- Hopes for r the future
- Bible study insights
- Prayers
- Thanksgiving

Don't feel you have to do it everyday but do it often enough for it to be a key part of your life.

Be Still
The spirit needs repose.

Just as the body needs rest to function optimally, the spirit needs quiet to function optimally. Too much noise and activity can crowd out the voice of God. God wasn't in the wind, the earthquake or the fire; He was discerned in stillness – 1 Kings 19:10-12. Psalm 46:10 says 'Cease striving (be still) and know that I am God'; is it possible that we can only know God when we find time to be still?

Whatever you do, make time in your schedule for moments of stillness – a morning alone, a day at the park by yourself or a weekend at a Christian retreat centre once a quarter. Invest time in being alone with God. Intimacy is forged in private.

Meditate
The spirit needs reflection

We need chunks of unhurried reflection time to live effective lives and to be truly spiritual people. The words of God are valuable pearls; they are not to be glossed over.

Take time to think upon scripture, linger on words that jump out at you, think on them and let them sit on your heart and dislodge incorrect understanding. Consider the meaning and application of God's word in your life and how you will apply it.

Follow
The Spirit is the master

God wants to have His way in you. He wants daily to mould and shape you so you look more and more like Him. He will inspire change by His spirit in you through instructions in scripture, nudgings in your conscience, and various promptings in your spirit. Let Him have His way; as He tries to lead and direct you in these ways, be sure to yield - do not harden your heart or ignore His whispers.

Serve
The spirit is a servant

….let it do its masters bidding. When your spirit is Christ controlled, it desires to express the love of God to others in kind deeds and actions. Find something to do which blesses God and humanity, where the primary reward is not for you.

Ayo Alakija is a medical doctor by training. After years working for the United Nations in Fiji, she moved to California with her family and started TDA (*Transformational Development Agency*). She is dedicated to alleviating the pain and suffering of the poor and her work is a service borne of her faith. TDA is a non-governmental/non-profit agency committed to bringing empowering change globally-through the shaping of government policy, the development and implementation of poverty alleviation programs, and social and business entrepreneurship. She says 'Our primary sectors right now include health and family with a particular focus on women and children at risk'. In this capacity TDA is involved directly with orphanages, centre's and program's dealing with orphans, street children, child prostitutes and child soldiers'. A committed wife and mother, Ayo admits it's a challenge to balance work life and family life. Now that her daughter is a teenager, she travels extensively and say's she couldn't do what she does without the support of her husband and a great live in housekeeper.

Time/life management tips

-   At the beginning of each year, mark out your children's school schedule and sport commitments and honor them.
-   Nurture yourself spiritually (Ayo prioritises her two yearly spiritual retreats – one personal and the second, a leader's retreat at her local church).
-   Make sure that you make time for yourself - not as a mother, wife or leader but time for yourself personally.

Chapter 9

GET SOME REST
THE GIFT OF THE SABBATH

Cease striving (be still) and know that I am God– Psalm 46:10

Many 21st century Christians don't know what the Sabbath is, still others consider it something peculiar to the Seventh Day Adventist movement. But the Sabbath is one of our greatest gifts from God and something He desires we practice in perpetuity. It is ...

....a day devoted entirely to rest and worship of God

The spiritual significance of the Sabbath

The Sabbath is a sign between us and God

Ezekiel 20:20 says "Keep my Sabbaths holy, that they may be a sign between us. Then you will know that I am the LORD your God."

First of all God wants this set apart time of devotion and rest to be a mark of our relationship with Him, like a marriage ring that signifies a wife is set apart to her husband. I also find it interesting that the scripture seems to intimate that if we don't have a Sabbath we cant know God or that it is as we honor the Sabbath that we are drawn into really knowing Him. As we set apart a whole day week by week to rest and fellowship with Him, we create a platform for Him to speak to us regularly without distraction or hurry. Lastly I am intrigued by a God that chooses Sabbath as a sign of our interaction with Him; it shows what His true heart is for His children – devotion and rest.

> *...as a sign of our interaction with Him; it shows what His true heart is for His children– devotion and rest.*

The Sabbath is a sign of freedom

God instituted the Sabbath at a time of transition, as the Israelites were moving from bondage in Egypt into the promised land. Slaves have to work all hours but free men can choose when they work; thus the Sabbath was a sign of their freedom. The inability to rest is a sign of slavery. Ouch!

God is calling us to liberty once again. He's calling us to come aside and rest awhile- Mark 6:31. Jesus regularly took time out to rest and worship – Luke 5:16, Mark 6:31.

The Sabbath is a sign for witness

When we honor the Sabbath and make it a part of our lives- we become transformed by it and others notice it. It can be a great tool for witness as neighbors and work colleagues enquire about our set apart day we can share about a God who desires rest for His children.

The physical benefits of the Sabbath

The advent of the laptop has meant that we can work anywhere 24hours day; and many of us work very long hours. Many of us (myself included) live like we have more energy than God. Genesis 2:2-3 says that after 6 days work God rested. It's amazing to me that God rests, but we feel that we don't need to. God created the whole earth and had plans to implement for it yet he took the time to rest. If we are too busy to rest then we are doing more than God intended for us to.

Rest means not doing work of any kind (*including checking emails, taking work related calls, filing or housework*). It also means taking time to sleep, read, relax or just do nothing. I am sorry I had to define it but it was necessary because many of us don't even know what real rest means these days.

> *Rest means not doing work of any kind (including checking emails, taking work related calls, filing or housework)...*

Rest is good for you!

God instituted the Sabbath because rest is a key ingredient for productivity. We push ourselves hard and squeeze out rest in order to achieve more, but we are not aware that lack of rest is robbing us of the ability to perform optimally. Check out the article below on the power of rest (in this case, in the form of sleep).

Benefits of Sleep

Mark Stibich, Ph.D. reports in an article [16]

There are other factors that make sleep absolutely necessary to life. Sleep is important for concentration, memory formation and the repair of damage to your body's cells during the day. Chronic lack of sleep increases the risk for developing obesity, diabetes, cardiovascular disease and infections.

Researchers do not know exactly why people need sleep, but we do know that lack of sleep can kill. In research studies, rats normally live two to three years, but if rats are totally deprived of sleep, they only live about five weeks. They also develop sores, their immune systems do not work well and their body temperature drops. Humans deprived of sleep for long periods begin hallucinating and develop other mental problems.

When people do not have enough sleep, they cannot concentrate well the next day and have problems forming memories. Researchers believe that during sleep, neurons can shut down and repair any damage done during the day. Without these repairs, the neurons may not function correctly due to a buildup of waste products. Sleep also seems important for the formation of memories.

Important hormone production is regulated during sleep; in children, human growth hormone (HGH) is released during deep sleep. Insufficient sleep can affect hormonal balance in adults as well. Tissue repair also occurs during sleep, including repair to the daily skin damage done by UV light. Getting enough deep sleep will help your skin repair itself.

When we rest we return to our work
- with more physical vigor
- with greater mental clarity
- often with a new and better perspective

Getting rest

If you have a hard time resting, check out the possible reasons below.

Inability to rest can be due to
- Poor time management which means we always have work to do
- Giving greater importance to our work than we should.
- Over commitment
- Workaholism or perfectionism
- Improper internal drives that push us to work continuously
- Not wanting to be seen as lazy

If you find it hard to rest it's important to examine your schedule, commitments and internal drivers critically to assess the cause of it so that you can know what needs to be addressed. At a session on the Sabbath at a pastors conference I attended with my husband another delegate mentioned that in his organisation taking a day off to rest was seen as lazy.pls don't separate, keep with previous For such a person, the first thing that needs to be addressed is the organisational mindset that he has about rest. Once he can accept that it's not being lazy but actually wise to take a day off; he then has to consider whether he wants to remain part of an organization that requires him to work all the hours God sends.

Chapter 9

Ask yourself - what do I need to do get a Sabbath into my week?
Getting a Sabbath day into your week

- Choose a work free day, for most people that's a Saturday or Sunday.
- Sabbath days need to be prepared for. Ask yourself, 'What do I need to do the day before to ensure that the Sabbath can be totally free for devotion and rest?' You may need to cook meals, give the house a quick clean or jot down to-do's for the day after Sabbath so that you can enjoy your Sabbath day properly.
- Get the kids into Sabbath – a day free of playstations, computer games and TV
- (is that possible? I haven't tried it yet, just a thought!). Encourage then to spend that day reading, outdoors or cook together and enjoy board games as a family.

What to do on a Sabbath day

When I first started trying to practice the Sabbath I found it extremely difficult. After the first couple of hours which I would fill with bible study and devotion I didn't know what to do with myself. I was tempted to pick up my laptop and surf the web but I knew that it was important to get away from all that. I wanted my Sabbath to be a step away from my regular routines and be a true time of rest. Here are a few tips for making the most of your Sabbath.

- Pray
- Study the bible
- Worship
- Read devotional or spiritual books
- Sleep
- Rest
- Restorative activities e.g. knitting, tending a garden, but no hard labour or housework
- Play board games as a family
- Meet up with an uplifting friend for late lunch
- Go for a walk with spouse, children or uplifting friends
- Do gentle exercises' like swimming
- Spend time outdoors- boating, visit a park
- Go visiting – museums or galleries

The most important thing to keep in your mind about the Sabbath is rest and restoration. If it's taxing or stressful in any way it shouldn't be part of your Sabbath.
I hope you will begin to implement the Sabbath day even if it is once a fortnight to start with – you'll be glad you did.

Chapter 10

Get Fit FOR LIFE

We make many grand plans but if we are not here or don't have the strength to accomplish them, what's the point? Our bodies are our only vehicle through life. It's the vessel or means through which we navigate and transact this life. Are you fuelling and looking after your body in a way that will encourage a long and strong performance? Take the quiz below to find out.

Healthy Eating Quiz[17]

Do you really know what eating healthily means? Find out whether you're a healthy eater or could improve your eating patterns.

You are running late for work and haven't eaten breakfast yet. Do you...

a. Skip it, you regularly do.
b. Make two pieces of white toast with peanut butter and eat them on the way.
c. Throw some sliced banana on a wholegrain cereal with skimmed milk and eat it before you go.

At work, it's time for your morning break. Do you opt for

a. A cup of coffee and a chocolate bar.
b. A cup of tea and two homemade oatmeal cookies.
c. A glass of water and an apple.

How many portions of fruit and vegetables do you eat on a typical day?

a. Less than 2
b. Between 3 and 5
c. 6 or more

When you grab a drink on the go, what is it most likely to be?

a. A fizzy soft drink.
b. A squash or a juice drink.
c. A bottle of water, smoothie or fresh juice.

You're heading for lunch with your colleagues. What will it be?

a. Bacon sandwich, coffee and donut.
b. Pizza topped with chicken and green peppers.
c. Grilled chicken, new potatoes and green salad.

How many glasses of water do you drink per day?

a. 0 to 2 glasses.
b. 3 to 5 glasses.
c. 5 to 10 glasses.

Tonight, you're ordering a takeaway with friends. What will you have?

a. Pepperoni pizza with extra cheese and garlic bread.
b. Sweet and sour pork with special fried rice.
c. Szechuan prawns with steamed rice.

What are you most likely to choose when picking a pud?

a. Cream donut.
b. Home made apple crumble with custard.
c. Fresh fruit salad with yoghurt.

Mostly As

You need to improve your diet! A diet like yours: high in fat, salt and sugar and low in fibre, wholegrain, fruit and veg is linked to obesity. Try small changes like more fruit and veg; ideally five portions a day. Aim to make one third of the food you eat, starchy food such as potatoes, pasta, brown bread and rice. Cut down on sugary drinks, sweets and cakes, and on processed meat products such as sausages and pies.

Mostly Bs

Try some small changes to your diet. First, try to eat five portions of fruit and veg a day. Dried fruit makes a great mid-morning snack. Base your meals on starchy foods such as pasta, rice and potatoes. Wholegrain cereals are a great source of fibre. Also, minimise your intake of processed meats such as pies and sausages, which are high in saturated fat. If you fancy a takeaway choose drier curries – such as tandoori or steamed Chinese food.

Mostly Cs

Well done, you're a healthy eater. Your diet is low in saturated fat, salt and sugar, and high in fibre, fruit and vegetables is helping to keep your heart healthy and protect against certain cancers. Remember, aim to eat two portions of fish a week, including one oily fish high in omega-3, such as salmon, trout, or mackerel. If you're a vegetarian, remember to get enough protein from nuts and seeds, beans and pulses, eggs, milk and soya.

If you have learned from the quiz that you need to get healthier, read onto find out how Bisi went from size 22 to size 8 and got fit!

276 pounds – who's counting?

Like most women today, I found the challenges of work, marriage and family overwhelming. Two rounds of childbirth had taken its toll on my body. I simply had too many important things to do and focusing on what I ate or getting some exercise was not a priority. Apart from the fact that I was tired all the time and didn't quite know why, I had no major complaints initially. Luckily living in California meant I was able to find semi-fashionable clothes to wear regardless of the weight I was carrying. As a matter of fact anything in as size 6 also came in a size 2X!

By July 2003, I had attained the colossal weight of 276 pounds. I ate what I liked, when I liked and didn't give exercise a second thought. Even after I wore out two chairs from the IKEA furniture store, I was still in denial. I blamed the badly made chairs. Who buys real furniture from IKEA anyway?

What prompted you to change?

I started to have back pains and the doctor suggested I try a variety of pain killers and when that did not work, I was sent for six weeks of physiotherapy. The back ache persisted and I began to find it hard to perform the every day tasks I had come to take for granted like dropping my eldest daughter at school, lifting the baby out of her car seat and doing my normal grocery shopping.

Eventually, my primary physician was kind enough to level with me. He was very honest about the fact that he would earn more money if he kept prescribing me pain medicine but he was certain that if I could simply change my lifestyle, I would find the

solution to my problem. To him my issue was simply that my back could no longer support my weight comfortably. It seemed the good Lord has created me with a small frame and here I was piling on twice the load it was designed to carry!

How did you lose the weight and get fit?

Being a goal-oriented person by nature, I was keen to find out what my weight ought to be

> *By July 2003, I had attained the colossal weight of 276 pounds. I ate what I liked....*

in conjunction with my height. I was shocked to find out that being 5"7, my weight should be somewhere between 126 and 154 pounds. I essentially weighed at least 120 pounds more than I needed to!

For the first time in my life (aside of visits to the doctor), I became keen to get a blood pressure reading. The results were not encouraging. My BMI (Body Mass Index) and cholesterol readings weren't great either. God had placed so many wonderful things in my

heart for me to do and I knew that if I continued living my life in the manner that I was doing, I would not be around to see any of it. Things had to change – for good.

My weekly exercise regime

I realised that just as it is important for me to fellowship with God, it is just as crucial that I eat right and exercise. I am busy like every other mother on the planet and there are a thousand and one other things I could do with my time, but I commit 2 hours at least three times a week to work out. It is such a habit now that if I don't, I start to feel ill. I found a form of exercise that I really love.-running. It's practically the only time I get to be alone so I cherish it. My mind can appreciate nature as I run and I

get to concoct new ideas in my head. Most of my best writing material comes to me as I run.

I started at the gym when I was at my heaviest. I would do 15 minutes on the treadmill and 20 minutes on weights. Slowly I started to walk 30 minutes effortlessly. As time progressed, I started to use the treadmill for running and ventured towards other cardio machines like the elliptical and bikes. I maintained my weight training throughout the process. This may be the reason why I don't have bat wings after losing about 120 pounds.

Now I do a total of one hour and fifteen minutes of cardio and twenty minutes of weight training three times a week at the YMCA gym next to my office. On my workout days, I start work at 8:00AM so I am out by 4:00PM and I head straight to the gym before I go home. I also run one day a week and on weekends.

My ability to maintain my weight has as much to do with my workout habits as my choice of foods.

My ability to maintain my weight has as much to do with my workout habits as my choice of foods. I eat just like anyone else but I eat a lot of foods that are low in calories.

My diet Regime

I still eat pretty much anything I like but within reason and definitely in moderation. My children can eat as much fast food as they like; because they are young, their metabolisms are still very much intact so they burn up most of it. Being

close to 40, I appreciate that the same does not apply to me! At the beginning of my weight loss, I did the Atkins diet which involves eating strictly protein only for the first two weeks. After the initial two weeks, I slowly introduced vegetables but avoided carbohydrates. I became an avid reader of food labels. I lost a good amount of weight in the first six months but my energy levels were low due to the lack of carbohydrates. I ditched the Atkins and started to eat from all food groups.

Seven years later, I eat pretty much everything. The only thing I definitely don't eat is red meat; instead I choose fish, chicken and turkey. I also implemented what I now call my "substitution methodology". Instead of soda, I choose water. Instead of palm oil, I try a little bit of olive oil. I fry food using olive oil. I also tend to eat spinach with everything rather than load up on carbohydrates. During my working day, I have a pro-biotic yogurt in the morning with a banana. I drink herbal teas a lot during the day – anything with ginger and lemon. For lunch, I tend to eat cereals with fat free milk and two pieces of fruit. Around 4PM, I eat two small tubs of yogurt. I drink at least 1 litre of water between 7am and 6pm and I avoid sugar as much as I can. Dinner usually involves oven baked chicken or fish with

lots of vegetables. I tend to make healthy choices when it comes to my snacks. I enjoy cakes and crisps but I buy brands like "Healthy Choices" and "Weight Watchers". I also eat a lot of almonds. My favorite snack is Hula Hoops though!

I have two free days where I eat anything I like – Saturday and Sunday. I find though that my system will react negatively to any food that is laden with fat.

Recommendations for other women desiring to become healthier

1. **Love** – You must love yourself enough to make the necessary changes. I have learnt over time to love me. You cannot love those around you if you do not first love yourself and treat yourself well. As the Japanese Kaizen principle implies, life must be one of continuous improvement. We are not designed to look worse for wear as time passes; like good wine, we are meant to look and feel better as we age.

2. **Commitment** – You have to be totally sold on the idea of getting healthier. Without total commitment to the change in lifestyle, success will continue to elude you. I must exercise at least four to five times a week-no excuses.

3. **Patience** – It probably took a while to get to the unhealthy spot you are in right now. It will probably take twice as long to get you out of the hole you've dug yourself into! Be patient with your body. Even when you cannot see the scale move, things are changing in your head and in your mind. Exercising and eating properly takes some getting used to. There is absolutely no magic here if you are to do things right.

4. **Support** – It is important to support yourself with people who appreciate what you are trying to do. My greatest supporters are my daughters. I remember when I was training for the Race for Life, I suddenly found myself surrounded by the food and exercise police!

> *Probably took a while to get to the **unhealthy spot** you are in right now. It will probably take twice as long to get you out of the hole you've dug yourself into! Be patient with your body.*

5. **Be a goal setter with regards to your health and weight.** Know what you weigh as and what you ought to weigh. Find out your BMI. and your cholesterol level, specifically your LDL (low-density lipoprotein) which is the harmful type of cholesterol.

6. **Re-order your life and priorities.** Ask yourself what quality of life you want for yourself and your family. When you are a parent, like it or not, your children are watching your health habits! I am at a point now where I exercise simply because I want to be around for as long as I can for my children. Most importantly, I want to model a healthy lifestyle for them. I totally get the fact that Almighty God holds the lives of men in his hand but I also know that my body is the temple of the Holy Spirit and I must honour the Lord with it.

7. ***Exercise***. Find time in your schedule to work out for thirty minutes to an hour at least three times a week.

8. ***Make healthy food choices.***

   a. Don't deprive yourself unnecessarily. Going on a hunger strike does not work because you cannot do it indefinitely. It's much better to eat nutritious food in the right quantity.

   - Avoid foods with high salt or sugar content
   - Avoid oily and fatty foods
   - Watch your carbohydrate intake (small quantities of pasta and rice)
   - Leave out red meat and eat more chicken and fish
   - Get plenty of vegetables and fruit in your diet
   - Replace full fat milk with skimmed milk
   - Go for wholemeal instead of white bread
   - Replace other oils with olive oil
   - Replace soda (fizzy drinks) with water.

GET WISDOM

No book on life management is complete without reference to the first ever, 'have it all' female — the Proverbs 31 woman. She stands as an icon even for 21st century woman. She ran a business, made time for charitable work and kept a marriage and home together — now that's a woman worth emulating and celebrating. Read her bio below.

A good woman is hard to find,
and worth far more than diamonds.
Her husband trusts her without reserve,
and never has reason to regret it.
Never spiteful, she treats him generously
all her life long.
She shops around for the best yarns and cottons,
and enjoys knitting and sewing.
She's like a trading ship that sails to faraway places
and brings back exotic surprises.
She's up before dawn, preparing breakfast
for her family and organizing her day.
She looks over a field and buys it,
then, with money she's put aside, plants a garden.
First thing in the morning, she dresses for work,
rolls up her sleeves, eager to get started.
She senses the worth of her work,
is in no hurry to call it quits for the day.
She's skilled in the crafts of home and hearth,
diligent in homemaking.
She's quick to assist anyone in need,
reaches out to help the poor.
She doesn't worry about her family when it snows;
their winter clothes are all mended and ready to
wear.

She makes her own clothing,
and dresses in colorful linens and silks.
Her husband is greatly respected
when he deliberates with the city fathers.
She designs gowns and sells them,
brings the sweaters she knits to the dress shops.
Her clothes are well-made and elegant,
and she always faces tomorrow with a smile.
When she speaks she has something worthwhile to
say,
and she always says it kindly.
She keeps an eye on everyone in her household,
and keeps them all busy and productive.
Her children respect and bless her;
her husband joins in with words of praise:
"Many women have done wonderful things,
but you've outclassed them all!"
Charm can mislead and beauty soon fades.
The woman to be admired and praised
is the woman who lives in the Fear-of-GOD.
Give her everything she deserves!
Festoon her life with praises!

Proverbs 31:10–31, The Message
Translation

The Proverbs 31 woman has been a role model to me all my Christian life- the kind of woman I want to be and time and again I draw wisdom, strength and inspiration from her life. From her I learnt that we are not supposed to do it alone – the wise learn from those who have gone ahead. It's important to support yourself with wells of wisdom. Below I outline various wells.

Mentors

My husband often says more is caught than taught. What that means is that you learn more from observing things being done than being taught how to do it. That's the benefit of a mentor – you learn by seeing them operate and if it's a close mentor (as opposed to a distant mentor – like the Proverbs 31 woman), you can also learn from them through talks and questioning. There is no better way to catch someone's spirit/attitude than by being with them – it rubs off on you! I have been tremendously blessed in ministry by 2 women who I had the pleasure of getting close to – Pastor Bimbo Odukoya and Pastor Ify Irukwu. By observing them and asking questions I gained wisdom about priorities, relating to my husband, managing ministry and family life. Even though they are now both dead, their lives still speak to me.

As mentioned above there are different types of mentors.

Close mentors – women you admire who have more experience than you in a specific area that you know and have a relationship with. You can meet and talk with them and gain direct access to their wisdom and life.

Distant mentors – women you admire who have more experience than you in a specific area that you have never met. You gain wisdom from these women by reading books they have written, watching or listening to messages they have preached or shows they have been on. I listen to a lot of material about pastor's wives; I have been tremendously blessed by the experiences of pastor's wives who lived in the 1800's, centuries before I was born. My distant

mentors include Susanna Wesley (mother of John Wesley), Clementine. Churchill (wife of Winston Churchill), Kay Warren (pastors wife and Aids activist), Michelle Obama, Michelle McKinney Hammond (for her prolific writing and example to mature single Christian women) and Kay Arthur (renown bible teacher).

There's wisdom all around you if you'll look for it. Seek out mentors – you need them. If there are none around you in the flesh, seek them out in books, magazines, Cd's – find them somehow!

Things to look for in a mentor

- Life experience and success in an area you desire to grow
- Integrity in their personal lives (as much as that is ascertainable)
- Good moral character

Good friends

Friends are an important key to successful life development. They are often the ones we go to for advice and bounce off life decisions on – so they should be people of worth and wisdom.

Friends also bring colour, fun and relief to life – at least they should! One of the things I look forward to most is lunch or a morning in a coffee shop with an old and trusted friend. It's an opportunity to catch up, laugh, review our lives and even get free therapy! No one understands a woman like another woman – there are things we just get – no long explanations needed. I am so often re-energised for life through these times of communion with a friend or friends.

I have also gained life tips by observing friends. As a newly married woman I learnt how to cook many traditional African dishes by over the phone tuition of a good friend
(thanks Bunny – I owe you or my husband owes you)! It was after a holiday where I observed a friend who had allotted household duties to her daughters that I learnt my sons weren't too young to help around the house. I learnt about encouraging good behavior in my children by using charts rewarding with points and stars from a member of our church. There's a lot you can pick up from friends –choose those you can learn good things from.

Books/ Bookshops

Bookshops are a treasure trove of wisdom on just about anything. Its mind expanding and life changing for various reasons.

- It's a good place to find out what's current – it's a good place to keep a pulse on what's going on in society in various arenas.
- It's a place to change and improve your life – go to the self help section and you can learn how to lose weight, cook, write a novel and do just about anything.
- It's a place to develop your business acumen – go to the business section and you're set to go.
- It's a place to travel the world – from an armchair, get a beautifully illustrated travel book and you can go anywhere in your mind.
- It's a place to inspire the next generation – my children are avid readers because we regularly had family outings to bookshops and they grew up surrounded by books.
- It's a place to gain wisdom on just about any area of life.

A bookshop visit should be a mandatory excursion every couple of months at least – we make it a family visit and you should too.

Conferences / Seminars

Conferences and seminars are great ways to get wisdom in specific areas. I have never attended a conference and left without at least one nugget of wisdom or tip that was useful. Conferences are great for

- Meeting potential mentors
- Getting wisdom / life tips in an area
- Networking – making new contacts/friends who have an interest in the same field
- Brushing up your expertise in a certain area
- Learning what's new in a particular field
- Being reenergized/inspired in some area of your life

Get a copy of magazines or bulletins or visit websites that advertise conferences in the fields of your interest. Try and attend at least one every 3-6 months.

Study the Scriptures

There is a fountain of inestimable value, from which all life springs. That fountain is open to you every day – the word of God. Learn to drink deeply from it and with time you will be filled with the wisdom of God. I am often amazed at how much wisdom the bible has for life for us, even today. In it you'll find guidance on

- Marriage
- Parenting
- Money management
- Healthy eating
- Wise speech
- Relating with authority figures
- Civic duty
- Relating with neighbors
- Purpose
- Wisdom
- Excess/Gluttony and moderation
- Becoming a person of character
- Righteousness
- True love
- Eternal life/life after death

....the list is endless- start your journey to wisdom. Pick up a bible today.

Get a copy of magazines or bulletins or visit websites that advertise conferences in the fields of your interest.

MAKE TIME FOR LOVE

Luther Vandross sang '*There's nothing better than love*', but the bible had said it earlier in 1 Corinthians 13.

If I speak with human eloquence and angelic ecstasy but don't love, I'm nothing but the creaking of a rusty gate. If I speak God's Word with power, revealing all his mysteries and making everything plain as day, and if I have faith that says to a mountain, "Jump," and it jumps, but I don't love, I'm nothing. If I give everything I own to the poor and even go to the stake to be burned as a martyr, but I don't love, I've gotten nowhere. So, no matter what I say, what I believe, and what I do, I'm bankrupt without love. ......we have three things to do to lead us toward that consummation: Trust steadily in God, hope unswervingly, love extravagantly. And the best of the three is love.

1 Corinthians 13:1-3, 13
The Message Translation

We are made for love. All of our lives are spent searching for it whether we know it or not. When we work all the hours God sends to earn a certain salary or gain a job title that says we are something, or when we search for significance and accolades in fame or notoriety of some sort – what we are really looking for is love. We want to be esteemed and valued. To be loved is to have value or meaning to someone.

And our lives are miserable without love. Human beings need love and affection to thrive. Dr Greene[18] writes 'Research shows that some children will fail to thrive despite adequate calorie absorption simply because of extreme neglect. Children who are not hugged, held, and cared for don't grow. This has been clearly demonstrated in orphanages where the adult-child ratio is very low. Even if these children are being well nourished, they often fail to thrive, simply because they lack personal care'.

Another report[19] says "Hugging is powerful. Hugging releases oxytocin, the brains bonding chemical. Studies going back as far as the 1930s have shown that people who did not receive adequate cuddling and touch as newborns later suffered both mentally and physically, even if all other basic needs were met. Others have shown that old folks who don't get hugs may become senile faster and die sooner."

How high a priority have you given love? Are you too busy working to make time for love? You know what they say, 'All play and no work makes Jill a dull girl'. Get some love in your life.

Your husband

If you are married – create time to spend with your husband regularly. Relationships require time investments. Find out what fills your husbands love tank regularly and make time to fill it regularly. Work and household chores can so easily fill up our lives that we neglect the most important things and wonder why our live are lacklustre.

Have a regular date night – once a week or fortnight

- A date night is a kid free time-get a babysitter or have it while the children are in bed.
- Go out to dinner and catch a movie or if finances are tight – make a special meal and rent a DVD.
- If you are eating in, set the table and have a meal and chat before you watch the movie- it's important to make time to connect.
- Make the room you are watching the movie in pleasant - light candles and fragrance the room.
- Sit close to each other as you watch the movie.

Retire to bed early - It's great to get to bed early once in a while just to catch up and talk with each other.

Touch often – touch is an important part of wellbeing and feeling loved. Get into the habit of holding hands, hugging and touching each other as you go through the day together as a couple. It makes a difference.

Write it down – send texts and cards expressing your love every so often- it's nice to be reminded that one is loved.

Say it – to their face. It's nice to be told you are loved.

3 things I resolve to do to show more love to my husband

1 ....

2 ....

3 ....

Your children

Children need our love desperately - give it lavishly. We are liberal with kisses, hugs and verbal declarations of love in our household. We often tell our children how much they mean to us and how special they are. They need to hear it –it builds their esteem and sense of value. My husband and I never want them to question how important they are to us.

Quality time – our kids love it when we spend time together, whether it's watching reruns of Fresh Prince of Bel Air or playing monopoly; they tell us that they enjoy that time with us.

Family trips – are a must and needn't be expensive. Whether it's a trip by car within the country for a weekend getaway or boarding a plane for more exotic climes, it's an opportunity to bond as a family. Away from work and regular routines we get to spend more time with our children, hear things that the busyness of everyday life fazed out and just enjoy them as people. We always laugh and come back with great memories and family anecdotes to keep us going for a few more months.

Attend school concerts and events

As an 11 year old in boarding school in England I used to dread school events where parents were invited because mine were never there (they were back home in Nigeria and could hardly be expected to fly down for 1 day). I know how I used to feel so I make it a priority to always be there at my son's school functions and have discovered how important it is to them also. They know the only reason we are there is because of them – we haven't come to see the other kids', we have come to see them; that makes them feel valued.

Celebrate birthdays and key events – buy a cake, make a nice meal and enjoy quality time together. Kids love birthdays (especially the part when they get gifts)! We also went out as a family to celebrate our son's entry into secondary school – it was a milestone and worth celebrating. He was chuffed because he got to choose the restaurant.

---

3 things I resolve to do to show more love to my children

1 ....

2 ....

3 ....

Friends and extended family

Friends and family also need to know that they are loved by us. I have a friend who regularly expresses her appreciation of our friendship through cards and handwritten notes- it is always touching to receive one. A thoughtful little gift every now and then or a 'I miss you my friend, lets catch up' message on Facebook is nice and goes to reinforce the friendship.

Invest in friendships with
- Lunch dates (sometimes with each others husbands if you are both married)
- Trips to the cinema or theatre together
- Prayer times together
- Encouragement chats
- Fun days window shopping

I confess I am not great at calling family members since they are all in Africa and I live in England; but my family and in-laws know how much I love them and my occasional texts let them know I am thinking of them. When they breeze into town, they stay over and we catch up over late nights filled with food and laughter. The great thing is when the chips are down we know we've got each other's back.

3 things I resolve to do to show more love to my friends and family members

1 ....

2 ....

3 ....

Receive His love

The greatest love of all, contrary to what the popular song says, is not learning to love yourself - it's learning to receive His Love. So often our lives are painful because we don't know how fiercely we are loved by God. I have vacillated between being convinced of it and doubting it. But the times when I am sure are like no other. Surety of God's love brings a peace and confidence regardless of whatever situation we may find ourselves in and assures us of our value regardless of our bank balance.

I think many Christians know in their head that God loves them but they are not assured in their hearts about the very personal care and love God has for them as an individual, foibles and all. I can only begin to feel it when I think about the love I have for my children — a fierce, protective and sacrificial love regardless of their flaws and failings. To know that God's loves us like this (we are His children after all) is life changing and affirming. Exploring the love of God in depth is beyond the remit of this book, but I encourage you to meditate on the following scriptures and I pray that you may begin to apprehend his love for you experientially.

Scriptures to meditate on His love for us:

- Psalm 139:14
- Deuteronomy 32:10, Zechariah 2:8
- Jeremiah 31:3
- John 3:16
- Romans 8:31-39
- Galatians 2:20
- Ephesians 2:4
- 1 John 4:10
- Psalm 91:4

I have struggled to accept God's love for me because

....

....

....

....

....

3scriptures that let me know I am loved by God.

Write them down and personalise it e.g. Bimbo is fearfully and wonderfully made by God.

1 ....

2 ....

3 ....

Love God

It is important to receive His love, because unless we do I think its hard to love Him back, and that is our calling – to love God (Matthew 22:36-40). It is hard to love a God who does not love us – who seems hard, cold, distant, uncaring. I believe it was Martin Luther, the reformist who said he could not love a God who seemed to delight in the abasement and suffering of His creation. It was only when Luther began to study the scripture enquiringly that He ran into a God of mercy and love he could readily embrace. It is only when we take time to study the word and discover His true nature and character and His love for us that we are in a place to respond to Him in the way that He deserves – with applause, gratitude and a devoted love.

Reflection

....

....

....

....

....

....

....

....

Footnotes

[1] Trends in female employment 2002. Melanie Duffield, Economy and Labour Market Division, Department for Work and Pensions

[2] The 2005 Time Use Survey, Office for National Statistics

[3] The 2005 Time Use Survey, Office for National Statistics

[4] Trends in female employment 2002. Melanie Duffield, Economy and Labour Market Division, Department for Work and Pensions

[5] The 2005 Time Use Survey, Office for National Statistics

[6] Dr Brent Bost as recorded in article by Robin Yapp in the Daily Mail, 30/5/05.

[7] Married only at the weekends? A study of the amount of time spent together by spouses-Reg Gatenby, Office for National Statistics

[8] Married only at the weekends? A study of the amount of time spent together by spouses-Reg Gatenby, Office for National Statistics

[9] http://longevity.about.com/od/sleep/a/sleep_benefits.htm.

[10] Research quoted in Dual Career Couples - Facing the "Stress of Success"- How Families Cope Part ITop of Form by Beverly Baskin, Ed.S, MA, LPC, MCC, NCCC

[11] Workingmoms.com

[12] [2] Attitudes to household chores, 2000-01, United Kingdom survey ONS as reported in article 'Jobs About The House-Household chores still women's work?' 2003 ONS

[13] [2] Attitudes to household chores, 2000-01, United Kingdom survey ONS as reported in article 'Jobs About The House-Household chores still women's work?' 2003 ONS

[14] Questions 1 and 11 taken from Pete Scazzero with Warren Bird, The Emotionally Healthy Church (Grand Rapids: Zondervan, 2003).

[15] Research by sociologist Dr Caroline Gatrell of Lancaster University as reported by Kate Hilpern in The Guardian, Saturday 2 February 2008

[16] http://longevity.about.com/od/sleep/a/sleep_benefits.htm.

[17] Culled from www.nhs.org.uk. Find out more about eating healthily by visiting http://www.nhs.uk/Livewell/Goodfood/Pages/Healthyeating.aspx

[18] http://www.drgreene.com/qa/possible-causes-failure-thrive#ixzz11ChbmeMK

[19] http://parenting.families.com/blog/dont-stop-hugging-your-teenagers